BLUE
Banner
BIOGRAPHIES

BEN SIMMONS

Kerrily Sapet

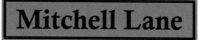

PUBLISHERS

2001 SW 31st Avenue
Hallandale, FL 33009

www.mitchelllane.com

First Edition, 2020.
Author: Kerrily Sapet
Designer: Ed Morgan
Editor: Lisa Petrillo

Series: Blue Banner Biographies
Title: Ben Simmons / by Kerrily Sapet

Hallandale, FL : Mitchell Lane Publishers, [2020]

Library bound ISBN: 9781680204971
eBook ISBN: 9781680204988

PHOTO CREDITS: Design Elements, freepik.com, Getty Images

Contents

An Aussie Legend

GUESTS at the National Basketball Association (NBA) Awards show had finished dinner and polished off the chocolate peanut butter cupcakes. Now they waited. Who would win the biggest award of the night? The presenters paused, then announced, "The 2018 Rookie of the Year is… Ben Simmons."

Simmons smiles for a picture after winning Rookie of the Year during the NBA Awards Show on June 25, 2018.

On his way to the stage, Simmons embraced Donovan Mitchell of the Utah Jazz. The two had been in a hot race for Rookie of the Year, along with Jayson Tatum of the Boston Celtics. In a landslide victory, Simmons won 90 out of 101 votes. He was the first Australian to be named Rookie of the Year.

"I broke my foot last season and I wasn't able to play," Simmons told the swarm of reporters. "So, to be on the floor and accomplish a childhood dream has been amazing for me."

Making it to the NBA had long been Simmons' goal. At seven years old, he made himself a to-do list, writing "Play in the NBA" at the top. Achieving his dream had required years of hard work and overcoming injury.

Two years earlier, Simmons was the No. 1 overall draft pick—chosen by the Philadelphia 76ers. Expectations were high. But before the season even started, Simmons broke his foot. He spent a long, frustrating year on the sidelines.

Coaches, players, and fans had wondered if Simmons would be worth all the hype after sitting on the bench for the entire season. "I came to the States when I was 15," Simmons said. "Nobody knew who I was. So, I feel like I'm back at that stage and I've got to prove myself again, which is fine. I'm looking forward to that part."

In Simmons' NBA debut, he blew everyone away, notching 18 points and earning 10 rebounds and 5 assists. "He's a monster on both sides," said teammate Robert Covington. "He doesn't even realize how good he is just yet." For the rest of the season, Simmons dominated the court. He fired long passes like a quarterback, and made all-out drives to the net.

Simmons was the first rookie with 1,000 points, 500 rebounds, 500 assists, 50 blocks, and 50 steals in a single season. With 12 triple-doubles (scoring double digits in points, rebounds, and assists in one game), he passed Michael Jordan's rookie triple-double total and stood second only to Hall-of-Famer Oscar Robertson.

That he was named Rookie of the Year was no surprise. He had taken the NBA by storm. Ben Simmons was becoming a basketball legend.

CHAPTER TWO

Boy from Down Under

ON JULY 20, 1996 Benjamin David Simmons was born in Melbourne, Australia. Images from the Olympic Games in Atlanta, Georgia, halfway across the world, had flickered on the television in the hospital room. Ben was born during a celebration of the world's best athletes. "I didn't think it was a sign at the time," said Ben's mother, Julie. "I think it was a sign now."

Basketball was in Ben's blood. His father, Dave, had moved from New York to Australia to play professional basketball with the Melbourne Tigers. When Ben's parents met, Julie was divorced with four children—Melissa, Emily, Liam, and Sean. Dave and Julie had two more children—Olivia and Ben. Ben, nicknamed "Benny," was the baby of the family.

Everyone in Ben's family played sports. Before Ben could walk, his brothers and sisters were rolling a basketball to him. A few months after Ben started walking, he was running and dribbling the ball. "He was dribbling from his pacifier and dribbling the ball," said Dave. Ben was a natural.

Ben's family was close knit and competitive. Even board games turned into fierce contests. But competing on the court didn't come easily to Ben. "I never wanted to play in the games. I was kind of nervous and shy," he said. "I used to sit on the bench with my mom." Ben soon discovered his nerves disappeared on the court.

At seven years old, Ben was playing against twelve-year olds. He and his friend Dante Exum played on the Newcastle Hunters team. The two grew up playing basketball together, battling each other in video games, and having sleepovers.

Playing for the Australian Boomers, Ben takes on Tom Abercrombie of the New Zealand Tall Blacks at the Men's FIBA Oceania Championship on August 14, 2013, in Auckland, New Zealand.

Ben split his time between basketball and Australian Rules football, nicknamed "footy." In footy, players run, dribble, kick, and pass a ball to their teammates. They move the ball down the field to score goals. Players move fast or get tackled. Ben excelled at footy but decided to focus on basketball. What Ben learned on the field helped him on the court. "I always knew inside I wanted to play basketball," he said.

Boy from Down Under

When Ben was in ninth grade, he helped the Australian team win a silver medal at the FIBA Under-17 World Championship (FIBA is the International Basketball Federation). The next year, his team took home gold. "I knew that he was going to be unbelievably special," said Kevin Goorjian, Ben's coach. "The possibilities for him are endless."

Ben tested himself against the best players in the world his age at the Pangos All-American camp in California. Soon afterwards, he started receiving letters from schools in the United States. "From there on, I knew I had an opportunity to get there," Ben said. "But I wasn't sure how much of an opportunity I had, because there's so many other good players."

Ben decided to finish high school at Montverde Academy near Orlando, Florida, a school known for its basketball program. His brother, Liam, coached basketball in Louisiana. His sister, Emily, lived in Chicago. They would be nearby to help their baby brother. Although Ben's mother thought he was too young to go, years later she would say it was the best thing that ever happened to him.

Believing and Achieving

ON JANUARY 9, 2013, Ben stepped off the plane into the Florida sunshine. Montverde Academy was home to one of the top basketball teams in the country. The head coach, Kevin Boyle, had developed NBA players.

At first, Ben was homesick. He missed his family and favorite Australian foods—lamb and Four'N Twenty pies (small meat-filled pies). But Ben's biggest challenge was adjusting to a new style of play. "[Basketball] is a lot different in Australia," he said. "It's more of a team-organized thing, and here it's a lot of individual play. I'm learning I need to be more selfish and take over the game sometimes."

Ben could dribble with both hands and play all five positions on the court, but he still had much to learn. "You have to want to be as good as Kobi (Bryant), as Michael (Jordan), as LeBron (James) every time you step on the court," Boyle told him. "You want people to say he's the best guy I've ever seen." Although Ben felt overwhelmed, he learned fast.

Each year, for the next three years, Ben helped Montverde Academy win the High School National Tournament. He also earned the Morgan Wooten Award, given to a player who shows leadership and character. As a senior, Ben was named the best high school player in the nation.

Ben poses during the 2014 Spaulding Hoop Hall Classic on December 19, 2014, at the Naismith Memorial Basketball Hall of Fame in Springfield, Massachusetts.

Universities with legendary basketball programs recruited Ben. His choice—Louisiana State University—surprised everyone. LSU was not a basketball powerhouse. To Ben, it represented a challenge.

"Ben's a little crazy in that Ben doesn't want to play with the top five players in the country and win a championship," said Ben's brother, Liam. "He wants to go out and beat the Kentuckys and the Dukes, the North Carolinas of the world."

Ben also chose LSU because he would be closer to family. His godfather, David Patrick, was the team's assistant coach. Patrick had played basketball with Ben's father and had known Ben for years.

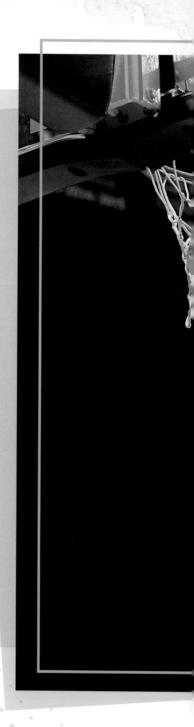

Simmons dunks during a game against the Kennesaw State Owls on November 26, 2015, in Baton Rouge, Louisiana.

Basketball fans packed the stands to see Ben Simmons. A sea of reporters followed him. "He had more pressure on him than any other player I've ever worked with," says Graham Betchart, the team's mental health coach.

Simmons' first game for LSU took place in Australia on a familiar court. On August 15, 2015, at the stadium where his father had played, he helped LSU defeat the Newcastle All Stars. Like his father, Simmons wore the number 25 on his jersey.

A month later, Simmons scored 43 points in one game—the most since Shaquille O'Neal had attended LSU. O'Neal called Simmons "the best player in the world." At the end of the season, Simmons was chosen as the NCAA Freshman of the Year.

Although he had only spent one year in college, he felt ready to play at the next level. On March 21, 2016, Simmons announced he would take part in the NBA draft. "It's once in a lifetime," he said. "There's a lot of people that don't make it. I'm just lucky to have the opportunity."

Simmons was named the No. 1 draft pick. Basketball fans around the United States and back home in Australia would be watching the draft. The NBA was waiting.

Simmons reacts to a dunk against the Kentucky Wildcats January 5, 2016 in Baton Rouge, Louisiana, a game his team won 85-67.

CHAPTER FOUR

Learning Patience

ON JUNE 23, 2016, the Philadelphia 76ers chose Simmons as the first overall pick in the draft. He was the only college player ever to be the first pick without playing in an NCAA tournament. His childhood dream had come true.

Simmons was excited to work with the Sixers' head coach, Brett Brown. Brown had coached Ben's father and Australia's Olympic basketball team. After Simmons signed a multi-year, multi-million-dollar contract with the Sixers, he signed a $20 million advertising deal with Nike. Simmons knew everyone expected him to be a star.

Simmons gets advice on the court from Brett Brown, the Sixers' head coach and a fellow Australian.

"There are rocky waters ahead as a superstar athlete," said Luc Longley, one of Simmons' former coaches. "But he's heading out on a big, exciting, dangerous, rewarding trip. There is so much for him to learn and do, so much work to put in."

Simmons got to work. While playing in the NBA Summer League, he impressed his teammates. "The stuff I've seen him do just training, it almost seems like it's not fair," said Amir Johnson of the Sixers. "He's just an unbelievable athlete and an unbelievable scorer and an unbelievable passer."

As the summer continued, Simmons grew stronger and more confident. But in the final training camp scrimmage, he rolled his right ankle and fractured a bone in his foot. He needed surgery and would miss part of the season. "It's like a punch in the stomach," Brown said.

A few months later, the news got worse. Tests showed that Simmons' foot hadn't fully healed. He would be out for the rest of the season. He was heartbroken.

At the home games, Simmons sat on the bench and gave pep talks. "He'd come over and tell me to keep shooting, talk to me about keeping my confidence up," said teammate T.J. McConnell. "It sounds corny, but it would make a big difference."

Simmons chats with teammate T.J. McConnell, also a point guard for the Sixers.

Learning Patience

When the Sixers played their away games, Simmons watched from home, alone in his bedroom. The team lost 54 out of 82 games. He texted Brown during games—sharing his observations.

To keep his spirits up, Simmons bought board games, Legos, and Nerf guns. He also spent time with his pets. He had adopted a sick kitten, two cats that looked like miniature leopards, and a Cane Corso puppy that would grow up to be 120 pounds. With too many animals for his apartment, he found good homes for those pets and bought a bulldog.

Simmons' first year in the NBA was not what he'd hoped. "I want to go in and make sure everybody remembers my name," he had said. People now knew his name, but could Simmons live up to his potential?

Star Sixer

AFTER A YEAR on the sidelines, on October 18, 2017, Simmons made his NBA debut. As the point guard for the Sixers, he ran the offense and was one of the team's best dribblers and passers. Although the Sixers lost to the Washington Wizards, Simmons scored 18 points.

Simmons drives to the basket during a game against the Washington Wizards on October 18, 2017.

Four games into Simmons' NBA career, he scored a triple-double. The streak continued. Simmons set an NBA record as the first player to score at least 170 points, make 100 rebounds, and get 10 assists in the first ten games of the season.

Fans in Philadelphia loved Simmons. In January 2018, the team held an Australian Heritage night. Everyone received kangaroo T-shirts and ate Four'N Twenty pies.

Simmons gives his sneakers to a fan at the end of the game during the 2018 NBA China Games at the Shenzhen Universiade Center in China.

By the end of the season, Simmons had made and received more passes than any other player in the NBA. He was the No. 1 rookie in steals per game and in assists. Simmons helped the Sixers end the season with a 16-game winning streak—a new team record. To cap it off, he was named NBA Rookie of the Year.

Hall of Famers called Simmons a once-in-a-lifetime player. His athletic ability was like something out of a fantasy world. "Ben is incredibly rare," said Brown. "He is very much a unicorn when it comes to being just really different."

As a rising star, Simmons is adjusting to fame and fortune. People notice everything from his shoes to his personal relationships. He surrounds himself with his close family and friends. He lives with his brother, near his parents, and hangs out with other Australian NBA players, such as his childhood friend Dante Exum, who plays for the Utah Jazz.

To Simmons, being a star isn't just about footwear endorsement deals and Ferraris. He values helping others. "If you ultimately become the best player in the world, that's an amazing achievement," said Ben's mother, Julie Simmons. "But it's what you do with something like that when you get it. There's no point to any of this if you don't do something with your success."

Simmons helps others in many ways. At the holidays, he gives shopping money to needy families in Philadelphia. Throughout the year, he volunteers at basketball clinics for kids. "It feels good to know I can be a role model," he said. "It also helps me make the right choices." During the summers, he leads basketball camps in Australia, inspiring future players.

"You've just got to set your goals and work toward them because I can promise you not many people thought I would be the No. 1 pick when I was 13 years old in Australia," said Simmons. "Anything is possible, and you've just got to work towards your goals."

Simmons dunks over Kelly Oubre Jr. of the Washington Wizards during the second half of the game on February 25, 2018 at Capital One Arena in Washington, DC.

He has become a 6'10" basketball star. Born during the 1996 Olympics, Simmons is set to play for Australia in the 2020 Olympics. Until then, he plans to be on the court with the Philadelphia 76ers, practicing hard, racking up wins, and smashing records.

Timeline

1996   Born in Melbourne, Australia

2012   Invited to the Pangos All-American Camp

2013   Moves to the U.S. to attend Montverde Academy

2015   Named the No. 1 high school player in the nation
Attends Louisiana State University

2016   Chosen by the Philadelphia 76ers as the first
      overall draft pick
Breaks his foot

2017   Plays his first NBA game
Sets a record for points, rebounds, and assists

2018   Helps win 16 consecutive games
Named Rookie of the Year

Quick Stats

Total Games Played	111
Total Games Won	69
Total Games Lost	42
Total Points Scored	1,757
Total Minutes Played	3,733
Average Points Per Game	15.9

Find Out More

Articles

Dinjaski, Melanie. "Aussie Basketball Phenom Ben Simmons Adjusting to 'Crazy' College Life at LSU." Fox Sports, August 17, 2015. https://www.foxsports.com.au/basketball/aussie-basketball-phenom-ben-simmons-adjusting-to-crazy-college-life-at-lsu/news-story/6ca5b946ad8e92cd3ec5579fabdab7c0

McKay, Adam. "Ben Simmons Gives Back." Helping Hoops, August 29, 2018. https://www.helpinghoops.com.au/ben-simmons-gives-back/

On the Internet

Ben Simmons Stats
http://www.espn.com/nba/player/_/id/3907387/ben-simmons

Ben Simmons Details and News
http://www.nba.com/players/ben/simmons/1627732

Ben Simmons Videos and Articles
https://www.nba.com/sixers/content/search/?query=Ben%20Simmons

Works Consulted

Auerback, Nicole. "LSU's Versatile Ben Simmons has a Natural Position: Star." *USA Today*, June 22, 2015. https://www.usatoday.com/story/sports/ncaab/sec/2015/06/19/ben-simmons-lsu-basketball-nba-guard-forward-recruit/71257494/

Barnsley, Warren. "Ben Simmons Ready to Make an Impact in the NBA." news.com.au, September 27, 2017. https://www.news.com.au/sport/american-sports/nba/ben-simmons-ready-to-make-an-impact-in-the-nba/news-story/d9447f73d7efe17052df457944431a7f

Cronshaw, Damon. "Ben Simmons is a Unicorn." *Newcastle* Herald, July 25, 2018. https://www.theherald.com.au/story/5543930/big-ben-simmons-dubbed-a-unicorn-photos/

O'Neil, Dana. "From Melbourne to Baton Rouge, Ben Simmons Has Arrived at LSU." *ESPN*, November 4, 2015. http://www.espn.in/mens-college-basketball/story/_/id/14050003/from-melbourne-baton-rouge-ben-simmons-arrived-lsu

Rosetta, Randy. "Ben Simmons' Connection to LSU Remains Rock-Solid After an Explosive Summer." *Times-Picayune*, July 24, 2014. https://www.nola.com/lsu/index.ssf/2014/07/ben_simmons_story.html

Sharp, Andrew. "The Ben Simmons Injury and the Bigger Picture for the Sixers." *Sports Illustrated*, October 3, 2016. https://www.si.com/nba/2016/10/03/76ers-ben-simmons-injury-foot-fracture-sam-hinkie-bryan-colangelo

Thompson, Matt. "NBA or AFL? Aussie Star Reveals Tough Choice." afl.com, April 26, 2018. http://www.afl.com.au/news/2018-04-26/nba-or-afl-aussie-star-reveals-tough-choice

Weitzman, Yaron. "Here Comes Ben Simmons." *Bleacher Report*, October 10, 2017. https://bleacherreport.com/articles/2737726-ben-simmons-sixers-2017-interview

Woo, Jeremy. "LSU Recruit Ben Simmons Could be the Next Ambassador of Australian Basketball." *Sports Illustrated*, April 18, 2014. https://www.si.com/college-basketball/one-and-one/2014/04/18/ben-simmons-lsu-tigers-australian-basketball

Youngmisuk, Ohm. "Sixers' Ben Simmons Claims NBA's Rookie of the Year Award." ABC News, June 26, 2018. https://6abc.com/sports/sixers-ben-simmons-claims-nbas-rookie-of-the-year-award/3653742/

Index

About the Author

Kerrily Sapet is the author of more than 20 nonfiction books and numerous magazine articles for kids. She grew up playing basketball in the driveway with her father and enjoys rooting for the underdogs in the NCAA Tournament. Sapet currently lives near Chicago, Illinois, with her husband and two sons.